Swan's Island

Swan's Island

POEMS BY

Elizabeth Spires

Carnegie Mellon University Press
Pittsburgh 1997

Library of Congress Catalog Card Number 96-83413
ISBN 0-88748-249-X
Copyright © 1985 by Elizabeth Spires
All rights reserved
Printed and bound in the United States of America

First Carnegie Mellon University Press Edition, March 1997

Swan's Island was first published by
Holt, Rinehart and Winston, New York, in 1985

Some of the poems in this book first appeared in the following magazines:
American Poetry Review: *"Storyville Portraits" (part 2);* The Antioch Review:
"Letter from Swan's Island"; Fiction International: *"Song of Renunciation";* The
Missouri Review: *"Whodunit";* The New Criterion: *"Two Shadows";* The New
Republic: *"Sleeping in a Church";* The New Yorker: *"Mascara," "Waving
Goodbye";* The Paris Review: *"Second Story";* Partisan Review: *"Storyville
Portraits" (part 5);* Pequod: *"A Book of Hours," "Ocean City: Early March,"
"Storyville Portraits" (part 4), "Woman Weighing Pearls";* Ploughshares: *"The
Falling";* Poetry: *"Angel," "My Daughter," "The Playground";* Scarab Press:
"Young Girl on a Chair"; Southwest Review: *"Café Luna";* Virginia Quarterly
Review: *"Storyville Portraits" (part 3);* Yale Review: *"Storyville Portraits" (part
1), "Crazy Quilt."*

*I would like to thank the National Endowment for the Arts, the Ingram Merrill
Foundation, and the Maryland State Arts Council for fellowships in poetry that aided
in the completion of this book. I would also like to thank Goucher College for a
summer research grant.*

FOR MADISON

Contents

• This symbol is used to indicate a space between stanzas of a poem wherever such spaces are lost in pagination.

I

Angel

AMIENS CATHEDRAL

O spirit embodied, but without
need of body, made without artifice
by Mind and worked in stone,
what was your Maker thinking of?
Your face smooth and untroubled
as a newborn's, the brow cool
and the eyes blind, one finger
touching the air, most fair of elements.
All is appearance, you tell us,
wearing the weight of stone wings,
stone clothes, without complaining.
Perhaps you, too, once had a flaw—
a thought, no more than that,
less than angelic. In a second
of a second, you were restored
to innocence by a Maker omniscient
and kind. The thought was gone.
But you were someplace other than
heaven. And changed to stone.

Letter from Swan's Island

The island's dark tonight.
The radio crackles with static, news
of a blackout, the voice
coming through first loud, then soft,
as if a storm were moving
to cut all lifelines off. My one-room
cabin has a bed, a table, a chair.
Living this way, I understand better
that scene by an anonymous
illuminator: a row of monks
eating at a rough table, diagonals
of light slicing across the room
to fall, as if by accident,
on their simple meal. The black
and white tiles on the floor
a symbol of the formal repetitions
of the simplest life, or maybe
an oblique allusion to a paradox
of theology: the complementary nature
of good and evil. Is evil possible here
where everyone lives so individually
and nature appears to be neutral
toward everything but itself?
Some mornings I wake too suddenly,
the light on the wall
brilliant and unfamiliar, and wonder
for a moment, where am I?
I answer myself, my disembodied voice

high and far off
like what I imagine saints and martyrs
heard in moments of ecstasy: *Swan's Island.*
Lightheaded, I rise, make coffee,
settling into the simple ceremony
of another morning. Outside the sea birds
pick the clam flats clean, fly off,
returning late in the afternoon
looking for more to scavenge.
Good days, I swim in the quarry,
sun myself on the rocks, and plan
a diary. One entry: *I feel
this place to be a rough approximation
of heaven, the heaven of the lost . . .*
But then I wonder if a diary
would be superfluous and put it off.

Days pass here, weeks slip away,
and even when it isn't,
it seems to be Sunday,
irreal, subdued, the queer, slowed-down
feeling of late afternoon
spreading through the hours
of an entire day. Impersonal, yet benign,
the sun rains indiscriminately down
on everything, instead of singling out
particular objects, so that
even the rocks out by the tide line,

normally gray-brown, become *heightened*,
false, and I have to turn away.

Sometimes the lobstermen wave to me.
I must seem frivolous to them,
an *outsider*, with my pants rolled up
to the knees, standing knee-deep in water,
a shell or rock in my hands.
We have a code. I wave a white
handkerchief above my head,
they blow their foghorns back.
Once means the mail's in,
twice, a storm by afternoon,
three times, the weather
will clear by evening.
But really, after a month
in a place like this, there's no use
to wonder *why* the sea does this or that,
what time it is, or whether
the approaching storm will be a bad one.
If I think of anything here,
it's the peculiar way
the sea gets into everything,
softening the crackers I seal
in an airtight jar, rotting the armchair
where I sit in the evening,
looking into the evening's afterlight.
It smells peculiar, *damp*,

as if it had been tossed overboard
from a dory, thought better of,
and hastily retrieved.

I have a fantasy: to walk on water.
Not eastward, the Atlantic far out
scares me, but long, island-hopping
giant steps up and down
the coast the way as a child
I'd make my "two-legged" compass
walk the map. Walking to school
a thousand winter mornings,
I imagined each thought, each step,
an exercise in good and evil;
or, after confession, I'd cup
my hands around my breath,
saved for an hour, knowing I'd sin
again, the scars on my soul
whitening like the scars on my hands
where I burnt them on the stove.
Swan's Island. A world
existing side by side with yours,
where love struggles to perfect
itself, and finally perfect,
finds it has no object.
The waking dream's intact—
the world continues not to change,
and staying the same, changes us.

The Falling

It rains and it keeps
raining, and there is
no sound except the sound
of the rain falling,
a sound with small
silences in between,
like music we can't
understand, expecting
each moment to be
filled with something.

The sound does not
explain the trees,
the yellow trees,
whose leaves are falling
like the rain, so
silently, leaving me
at a loss, completely
at a loss, leaving me here
and you there and so much
unspoken between us.

Soon it will cease,
the endless falling,
so that the silence
will come to be a sound,
and the sound of falling
will recede, no longer
enclosing the trees,

each in its posture
of grief, whispering,
teach me how to live.

Crazy Quilt

Each night, eyes closed, I walk the crazy rows:
no up or down, no north or south
to guide me, I zigzag, dizzy and drunk,
my heart, like the quilt's, off-center.

The sun and moon, at odds with one another,
shine darkly from different corners.
Random stars point this way and that.
A dog barks. A calico cat meows.
An owl hoots, not unkindly, "Who? Who?
Who are you looking for?"
Before I can answer, it disappears.

A house, a heart, a tree.
This must be childhood, a road
leading through unreasoning, moonlit fields
I almost remember. The only rule is simple:
for each step forward, take one step back.

I find a piece of silk from my mother's
wedding dress, still gleaming whitely,
a tie my father used to wear.
Each thing I touch initialed and pieced-in
carefully, my birth, a wedding anniversary.
But something's always missing.
"Not for a child's ears," they said
when I asked, "Who's dead? Who disappeared?"

Each night I walk the quilt in circles,
retracing the past, waiting for morning

to call me back. "Mother, where are you?"
I call and call, my voice traveling
beyond me, echoing back. I hear her answer,
so near, so far within the quilt's
dark borders, "I'm here. I'm here."

My Daughter

AFTER A THEME BY
CARLOS DRUMMOND DE ANDRADE

Late in the afternoon, she sits with me,
trapped in the corner's shadows,
a thought that comes and goes,
dark hair unlike my own, dark eyes
that mourn the absent love between us,
her life a task of waiting she did not choose.
The light shines through her body,
her eyes fill with tears, but still she says
nothing, no, nothing at all. She waits
until the sun disappears, and then she goes,
taking my name with her, leaving
a silent space that words can never fill,
my daughter, the one I never had, who calls
to me so softly that nobody hears.

Mascara

FOR ANN

One eye swims into view, bright as a fish,
enlarged, and swiftly the eyelash lengthens,
grows, the eye pools to its own longing,
as you twirl the mascara wand and smile,
then frown, at what you see, shadowing
the eyebrow, the cheek's hollow, wishing
for what? I don't know. Over your shoulder,
I see my own face, unmasked, ten years apart
from you, an old moon looking at the new.
Then cheek to cheek, we stare for one
bright moment in the mirror, as close
as old injuries, forgotten but not entirely
forgiven, will allow. We share each other's
face, as sisters do. The mirror glows.

The Playground

Although
the moon is rising and the doors of the house
are locked against the darkness,
and pockets of leaves spin to no purpose
in the whirlwind, I get up
and dress myself, drawn by the shouts
of the children on the playground
playing tug-of-war and crack-the-whip,
the lines alive, *taut*,
as the smaller ones spin away, one by one,
into dark corners where nothing can save them,
and I join the game without a word to anyone,
caught in a line
snaking backward and forward
until it joins, like time, at either end
and mends invisibly,
the face of the child on either side of me
pale as a star
as each holds my hand tightly,
begging to enter the world and live a little while,
my body the instrument of passage.

We play
as the clock strikes
one, then *two*, then *three*,
encircled by light, outside the circle shadow,
and they make all the rules,
and I obey,
no thought to the waning moon

that turns the city gray, the world inverted
like a dream I'll wake alone from in the morning,
the bed's cold sheets
thrown off like so many obligations,
as they pull me toward them and I pull away,
the future bearing down so quickly upon us.

A Book of Hours

Skins are dyed with the color purple,
gold melts into letters, the books
are clothed with gems—and Christ
is left standing naked outside the door.
                                    —ST. JEROME

Bound in blue morocco, tooled in gold,
the book is small, untouchable,
each page framed by a border:
acanthus, columbine, thistle-on-gold,
and forget-me-nots scattered
abundantly in the margins,
profuse, startling,
the painted dragonfly a miracle
of *trompe l'oeil*, appearing
to have landed on the page
only a moment ago
when our backs were turned
to the open window. Inside each frame,
a scene from a saint's life,
in this case, St. Barbara
holding an open book of hours,
her pale, expressionless face
unmoved by what she sees, her soul
already saved, the moment of grace
taking place not, as we had expected,
in radiant surroundings but in dull light,
the illuminator turning our attention
from the present illusion—
sensory, bright, fluttering—
to the moment of salvation, and back again,
as if he were unsure himself,

torn between *vision* and immediacy,
the soul warring against the world,
or giving itself up in sweet surrender.

The book outlives itself, and us,
growing beyond
whatever meaning it held
to hold us in a meaning of our own,
bright enough to be blinding,
painfully distilled,
so that we look and look
unceasingly, in simple disbelief,
bound to an image of ourselves
as doubt is bound to faith.

And cannot look away.

Storyville Portraits

NEW ORLEANS RED-LIGHT DISTRICT, 1912;
A SEXTET OF PHOTOGRAPHS BY E. J. BELLOCQ

1

Legs crossed, in black-and-white-striped stockings
that startle the eye, obscene, yet oddly
funny, she sits with one elbow propped on a table
that holds an alarm clock and bottle of Raleigh Rye,
holding a half-full glass herself, her face half
in shadow. Her hair is pinned up, caught
in a black ribbon above her head; around her neck,
a locket on a chain. On the wall behind her, undecipherable
portraits of what she might have been, the faces of five
or six women trapped behind glass, peering
anxiously out at us, asking for something. But what?

She asks for nothing. She smiles, relaxed, but doesn't
look at us, or at the photographer, Bellocq, an odd, misshapen
man who only asks to take her photograph.
Well, each to his own. It's noon by the clock,
a "slow time." He's caught the decay in the room, its charm,
the way time eats away at everything: the edge of
the peeling rug, the stained wallpaper. Or has the print
simply begun its slow disintegration? We can't say.
She is the focal point, beautiful, unknowable,
conscious that the photo is a form of trickery, the trick
to survive, to be "acted upon"
as Bellocq bends over the black box, the world going
out of focus, narrowing, as he focuses in on her, the shutter
opening even as the "eye" closes, Bellocq, for an instant,
out of time, her willing instrument.

2

One looks away at once, frightened
at the way the mind denies the body,
the body denies it *is* a body,
erased, *gloved*, in a white leotard—
as if she were nude but featureless—
the eyes opaque, wary of self-
betrayal, as she leans back on the armless
chair, arms crossed behind her,
thrusting her body into the foreground
to breach a space between herself
and us with an invitation that is not
an invitation, the hatred unequivocal,
her only emotion a motion away from
anything that might save or destroy her.

Her aim? To fly
out of her body through void and space
to a place that is not a place,
neither warm nor cold, dark nor bright,
gray tabula rasa of the afterlife
where Time is an empty frame
she moves freely in and out of.
Afterward, the afterimage stays: light
rushing away from the white hourglass
of her body, the nights, the days,
a series of blunt enactments, briefly
imprinted on the retina: love's negative.

3

She could be anyone: a woman
pinned like a moth to a wall, the face
scratched out, no eyes to read
the fear in, the background *stripped*,
bare, as if she were cut out
of another context and placed *there*,
a man's hand shadowing the negative
in unimaginable rage against himself
and her, staring and staring
at the curving line of the torso,
then scratching out the face
and leaving a ripped black space,
so that suddenly she is no one,
a woman radically effaced.

Her arms, thin wings that cannot
fly, contrive the soul's survival:
the left, pulled down to waist-
level, hand clutched into a ball,
in counterbalance to the right,
impelled to reach upward
and draw a figure on the wall
small enough to be unnoticeable
until we bend closer and see
with a shock the soul transcribed:
chalk, blurred, a butterfly.

4

Left to herself, only herself,
she stares in the mirror,
her back to the photographer.
Inside: a room like her own
but one she cannot enter,
everything there inevitable,
implied, white chest
of drawers backed into a corner,
the illusion of the *other.*
A woman looks out at her,
her twin, her alter ego,
and asks the unanswerable,
the answer reflected in
the question: *How old am I?*

They reach toward each other,
testing the surface, two
halves of a whole, nakedly
objectified. *Who reflects who?*
thinks the woman in the mirror,
her life narrowing before her,
a series of identical rooms,
each smaller than the one before,
so that she grows smaller
and more terrified as she
follows herself into the future,
only one room visible at a time.
She looks no farther.

5

Her wish: to live in the body
as a visitor, mouth painted on,
breasts two cones of light,
legs closed against her sex,
and not a clue, not a sign
as she lies on the swirling wicker chaise
that she ever wanted anything but this.
A woman with a past but no future,
acquiescent to any mood,
who knows that acquiescence is her freedom.
The secret: to lie still, her hair
unfolding on the pillow, to lie still
and look at us until we understand
that look is our own conscience.

Tired of the pose, her left hand
moves, blurring the slow exposure,
ring flashing out, fingers slowly dissolving.
Body and soul, thought and emotion, the present
moment and hereafter: two sides of a coin
spinning so fast distinctions are useless.
Her eyes invite, *defy*, any hand
to touch her, knowing the soul,
intact, *whole*, subsists entirely
on the meager rations of the physical,
that flesh is permeable to Time,
her visible hand a claw of light and shadow,
as, alone and strangely generous,
she shares the slow death of her body with us.

6

Two faces: a woman and a dog
in an impromptu pose in a courtyard.
It's early morning; she's dressed
in pantaloons, a white smock
unbuttoned at the top, hair artlessly
pulled back, a little lipstick,
holding a black dog in her lap,
the soul shining through the eyes
of one, the other without a soul,
its eyes dark, round, and shallow,
seeing the outward world we see,
the lines and shadows of material
reality, only flattened out, colorless,
in two dimensions instead of three.

Depth. Color. Memory. *She*
sees things differently, choosing
the moment, or letting it choose
her—it doesn't matter—the choice
made easy if Fate and Free Will
are both illusory. She is happy
perhaps, but not in a way we know,
and probably she doesn't stop
to think so as she holds the dog's
body, the corporeal husk,
a shield, an offering to us,
believing, as she must,
There is no life but this one.

Young Girl on a Chair

A SCULPTURE BY GIACOMO MANZU

Refusing to see, having seen all,
the bronze girl sits, a scar
across one cheek,
eyes closed against the visible.
The grass, knee-deep, shudders
in the heat, bending to the slightest breeze,
as if she's in a field, an unmowed field,
not walled in, not enclosed,
as she is, as she must be.
Never, no never, will she
rise and walk among the others,
figures vague and dim as in a newsreel,
who shudder and bend
as time moves them to a place
they cannot apprehend. Time circles her.
Shadows fall and move
as the sun arcs
above her head and the traffic moves,
as pockets of leaves gather and spin,
as snow clings
to her shoulders, and the crocus,
hidden against spring, ascends.
And the birds
feed and cry in wonder at one
who sits so still
as night continually falls, and falls
again, and blindly,
she feels it on her skin, but feels it
as sensation, just as she feels

the dawn,
a chill, a sudden quickening,
and she the metaphor, the illustration,
beyond all knowing, knowledge gone.

Song of Renunciation

Nothing can be taken back.
No word. No act.

Nothing can be kept from harm.
No child. No man.

Good and evil. Black and white.
The devil laughs at opposites.

The saints, each one, said
in ecstasy:

I shall live in this world.
I shall live in this world

but not love it. Instead,
I shall love what I cannot

see, what I cannot hear
or hold close to me.

And committed, each one,
the sin of infidelity.

In poverty, we bear love's sins.
Uttering the same words again and again.

II

Second Story

How strange to be sitting in this room,
to be noticing the windows—clearer than air—
how they let in everything, the leaves,
the bright-colored leaves, hanging like bits
of paper from the trees, and the thin woman
across the street sweeping her porch—
though she swept it yesterday and the day before
and will, most likely, sweep it tomorrow—
and how strange to be thinking of you, always
of you, as the room changes imperceptibly, easily
moving from moment to moment, like a lover
whose infidelities are purely imaginary,
imagined by *you*, just as you're sure
the house might betray you, accommodating shadows
in your absence, sure that the room only
pretends to be *your* room, light climbing the stairs—
like an intruder or friend who left a long time ago—
pausing, changing its mind, going back down again,
as if the door were open and it could
come back anytime. Strange after so much time
to feel the same feelings, only stronger,
as the dust settles thickly on the tables,
and the afternoon shadows, unsure of themselves,
shrink into corners or lie on the floor,
and no letters arrive and the phone doesn't ring,
and the woman sweeping her porch casts
a cold eye up at you—the face in the second-story
window, the whorled face staring at the view—
goes into her house and shuts the door.

Waving Goodbye

The world bends us to its purpose.
In the public gardens, we found
a "gazing globe" balanced
on a waist-high pedestal,
a silver ball a foot in circumference,
reflecting sky and ground,
ourselves as we stood above it.
We stared into its depths,
as in a crystal ball,
our faces large and wild,
arms and legs unnaturally small,
as if a spell were on the world,
or, finally, we clearly saw the world
for what it was: too brightly
shining, circular, unadorned.

Trees bent toward us, mere shadows
of themselves, their shadows
more substantial than the trees themselves.
The sky at one o'clock
a milky white, light-filled,
yet without sun or cloud. And beds
of tulips rising from the groundswell,
each one a little mouth.
I knelt beside you on one knee,
caught up in walls of air
I couldn't touch or see, the outer world
around me wavering, as on a hot summer day.
•

We looked out to the future. Our future
selves. You stood dead center
in the globe and raised your hand to stop
the scene, your palm enlarging
until it dwarfed the tallest trees.
Then waving goodbye, we walked,
as a joke, backward and away,
farther and farther away—
the globe still gazing on us—
leaving ourselves behind
to live forever in that silver room,
to watch and spy on lovers like ourselves.

Ocean City: Early March

Along Ocean Highway, apartments rise up
to ten and twenty stories,
white, hallucinatory, defying the shifting sand,
the storm moving in off the Atlantic
that drives the rain, needlelike,
across the windshield so that we can't see,
so that we stop in Ocean City to wait the storm out
at the Dutch, the only bar on the boardwalk
open this time of year, all the concessions
boarded up, weather-beaten, closed against the season.

Last summer in violet light, kites
spiraled downward in loops, then up,
dragons and birds flying high above the boardwalk.
Ocean City. Haven of the lost and aimless,
with a ten-foot sand sculpture of Christ
illuminated by neon lights.
People on their way to Ripley's BELIEVE IT OR NOT
looked on in apathy, then wandered off,
their children begging for another ride
on the Avalanche or Safari.
Out, far out, at the end of a pier,
silhouetted against gray sky, gray water,
Morbid Manor rose up, Gothic and dreamy,
as children ran screaming from the exit door
chased by a ghost with a chain saw.
One child ignored it all; she lay with her face
pressed close to a knothole in the pier,
looking down, down, to the boiling black water.

"What do you see?" I asked,
but she didn't move or answer me.

Long, narrow, and dark,
the Dutch, with its shifting clientele—
from summer weekend pickups to Ocean City regulars—
allows for strangers. We order Irish coffee,
then two more, and use our change to play an arcade game.
Aliens, half an inch high, in green armor,
drop out of a glowing sky and quickly multiply.
Our backs to the storm, we play out
old anxieties, losing each game to time and starting over:
we must save what's being threatened and not ask why.

Sleeping in a Church

MILLVILLE, DELAWARE: AN OLD COUNTRY CHURCH

Free to us, not covered by the lease,
mice, mice in the walls,
that scamper back and forth
on the two-by-fours
all day and all night long; and a moth
with an eye on each wing
—beautiful but dead—
that blindly stares at the ceiling
where prayers, incorporeal but *real*,
hover and hover,
silently bumping into each other.
This church isn't used anymore
for praying: it's been retired,
restored and rented out
to summer people who push the pews
against the walls to make room
for the ping-pong table;
who leave us notes
about wasps in the shower
and occasional strangers who knock
on Sundays at the front door,
surprised to find tenants
in their nightclothes.
Each night, around midnight,
a cricket creeps out of the stove
to preach at us and the mice.
His two notes boom off the ceiling:
Get out! Get out!

You are not small enough!
You have no right!
We sleep well, despite the sermon,
but wake at 6 A.M., rubbing at gold dust
in our eyes. It's only the sunrise,
slanting through stained-glass windows
to fall at the foot
of our bed in colored squares.

Street Scene

Two acrobats, in red, in green,
cut out of cardboard, jointed & joined
at the hands, six inches high,
dance without thinking under the sky.
One bows at the waist & pulls
the other up, steps backward & falls
to its knees, proposing formally.
Off to one side, the sidewalk vendor smiles,
pleased that we'd like to believe
the little acrobats are *alive*, not tied
by trick or illusion to a lifeline.
He has a suitcase of their twins,
their faces, pale stencils of desire,
identical: they neither laugh nor cry.
Their balance is precarious. Unable,
in love, to unlock hands, they move,
they dance. They do not see us, eyes
locked into each other's narrow glance.

Espresso

The moon rises, a white cup filled
to the brim with black water, the delicious mud
of Baltimore Harbor ground finer and finer
by the slow tides of the Chesapeake River.
The night is dark and rich and thick, sweetened
by both just and unjust rewards, a rind
of bitter lemon, a spoonful of sugar stirred
slowly into a steaming cup of espresso.
Life quickly happens, the spirit a child who
begs to stay up all night, and will, recklessly
paying with the cold coins of tomorrow. Our empty
cups stare up at us, the day unaccountably
gone, spent easily, but to what purpose? We
have drunk the night and will not sleep till dawn,
our lives half over, only half begun.

Ghost of a Rose

*To let mee live, o love and
hate mee, too.*
　　　　　—JOHN DONNE

Instructing me in love,
a lover's metaphysics,
you bend toward the rose
so new that dew covered it
this morning, its white face
tightly closed, paling as you
push the head down and stroke
the spiked green throat
until the flower chokes
and whispers, *Hate love!*

Your face intent on mine,
you strike a match and watch
the flame touch, catch
each blanching petal, testing
the Metaphysicals' belief
in the souls of flowers—
bright Immaterials
freed only by fire—
our eyes crossed, locked,
in love's unloving paradox.

Hate love!
the burning spirit
whispers out of breath.
It's done. As thought
negates emotion, emotion

thought, my love negates
your hate, your hate
my love. Sight's gone.
The heart exposed
for nought: a burning rose.

Bread & Water

The long year after you left, walking
from room to room, for no reason.
On the worst nights, my body striped
by weightless bars of moonlight.
A trip south did me no good.
Walking the beach in January, I came upon
a mermaid, ribs hollowed out, one sandy arm
thrown over her face, who lay on a strip
of no-man's-land, tail curved in an ache
toward the water. The next day she was gone,
erased by the tide.
       "A great prince in prison lies,"
wrote Donne. I understood but would admit
to no one. Although I ate, I starved,
denied. My room: my cell.
My ration: bread & water.

Woman Weighing Pearls

The hand perfectly still, holding a scale
on which she weighs each pearl, no two
identical. The moment's still, still
and prescient, the spirit shaping itself,
layer upon layer, around the dark core.
The way, she thinks, *pain must form
the pearl. But not a human pain.*
Love's rounded walls are here, here
on the breathing sides of pearls,
worlds on which the soul prostrates
itself, must eat and sleep and dwell,
held dear and dearly paid for
with our lives, quick to disappear.
She wears the beaded years, choosing
one against the other, as we might choose
between words, their fine meanings.
      Already, the moment is decaying.

Whodunit

Like a photographer developing a photograph,
slipping the light-sensitive paper
into solution until the image rises,
clear as a piece of evidence,
day rises slowly out of dawn,
each tree dripping with mist, leaning
toward the house with mute, inarticulate
secrets, new leaves suffusing the rooms
with the green light of memory,
green's utter recall.

The day is a question mark,
unpredictable as the detective novel
you were reading last night:
a car on a hairpin curve skidding
toward a guardrail, a woman
pushed from a second-story window
who may be guilty or innocent.
The book lies facedown
on the table beside the glass of water
and the sleeping pills, open to the page
where you left off reading,
so that she falls and continues to fall
all night, silently screaming,
an unfinished, interrupted dream
with only one possible ending.

Below the yard is brightening,
long shadows lie like stains in the grass.

You sleep unaware I'm not beside you,
the sound of a pen scratching out
a message on paper, a car door slamming,
a shout, making their way
into your dreams, the first clues
that the day may or may not turn out
as you expected coming to you in sleep,
gentle, insistent, veiled.

Clue Sestina

One of us will die in a room
of this drafty mansion though I accuse nobody.
The truth, they say, is seldom black and white.
My idiosyncratic "sense of form" permits me to note,
however, certain departures, omissions in the story,
for instance, the disturbing fact that Miss

Scarlet, chronic insomniac, was miss-
ing this morning from her bedroom.
I took the secret passageway to the conservatory,
relieved, when I got there, to find no body.
Considerately, it seems, she's left a note
(which I've pocketed): *Dear Mrs. White,*

There's a scarlet stain on my white
evening dress. Could you get it out? Signed, Miss
Scarlet. P.S. Tell no one about this note.
Down the hall, in the dining room,
sinister Mr. Green and Colonel Mustard, an old Tory,
argue over the red herring. "One *must* produce a body

to prove murder!" shouts Mustard. Mrs. Peacock, a busybody,
bends to the keyhole, taking notes. "Why, Mrs. White!"
she says, embarrassed. She writes whodunits, has a history
of eavesdropping at closed doors. Perhaps she knows Miss
Scarlet's whereabouts? The door of the dining room
flies open. Mrs. Peacock drops her notes,

•

full of diagrams and unreadable codes, notes
riddled with darkening plum-colored stains. From a body?
"I think you had better come into the dining room!"
demands Green. "And you, too, Mrs. White.
All right, which one of you disposed of Miss
Scarlet? Quickly now. Let's have the entire story

before our time runs out." "Only *I* can finish the story,"
declares Professor Plum, entering unexpectedly. "Note
that I've been absent all day, along with our dear Miss
Scarlet. The tease! Does anybody
realize how she toyed with men? Do you, Mrs. White?
I forged the note." He looks around the room,

smiles, takes out a white revolver. "Our little story
ends, I'm afraid, on a tragic note. You'll never find Miss
Scarlet. Death is a very small room in which to hide a body."

Café Luna

Maybe because of the rain,
falling in sheets all day
between the narrow buildings
of Little Italy, the Café Luna's
plate-glass lettering, CAFÉ LUNA
(read from the inside out),
appears to be dissolving,
as if the words were written
in semipermanent ink.

The remarkable espresso machine,
solid brass, with a pair
of wings on top, sits behind
the bar looking as if it might
take off in flight. Be careful.
It will catch at your face,
distorting it, as water distorts
sound, so that the laugh
we just heard outside might
only have been a car backfiring.

A smiling man in blackface
walks in, carrying a battered
black suitcase, lettered
on one side in silver, *The Enchanter.*
He takes the table next to ours
and pulls three odd-shaped bottles
from the suitcase, labeled
Lucky Dream, Steady Work, Strong Love,
the liquor inside each

the color of, respectively,
absinthe, chartreuse, and amaretto.

Uncapping the first, he pours
one drop in a glass and drinks
it down, then weaves his way
to the jukebox, ignoring
the OUT OF ORDER sign taped
on the glass. He drops a silver
dollar in the slot, steps back,
and rubs his hands together
until his white gloves
glow, or seem to glow,
in the café's muted lighting.

Maybe the worm in the bottle
of absinthe is a prop,
maybe the room really *does*
slowly start to spin, lights
blinking on and off, as
the jukebox brightens
and begins to play "Moon River."
A quartet of voices rise
off the record, sirenlike,
words whirring together,
the gloved hands of the café's
moon-faced clock racing
toward midnight. Coins,
pens, and cigarette lighters
fly out of our pockets as

we grip the nailed-down table
and hold on for dear life.

And then, the song is over.
The spinning room slows down
and stops. The jukebox darkens.
The Enchanter's vanished,
picking our pockets but
leaving *Lucky Dream* behind,
half full, tipped on its side.
We watch it roll across
the tabletop, pause at the edge,
the greenish liquor dripping
drop by drop, then fall
with a crash, a broken bottle
all that's left of the night.

Outside the rain has stopped.
Another moon, in whiteface,
pauses between buildings
to look in at us—
impassive, disinterested—
effortlessly turning
the stones in the street
to silver. Enough of a sign
for us to stumble out of
the Café Luna, past stores'
Dream Merchandise, listening
for once to the moon's advice:
Go home now. You must go home.

Two Shadows

FOR MADISON

When we are shadows watching over shadows,
when years have passed, enough to live
two lives, when we have passed
through love and come out speechless
on the other side, I will remember
how we spent a night, walking the streets
                     in August, side by side,
following two shadows dressed in long gray coats,
unseasonable clothes they didn't seem to mind,
walking so easily, with easy stride,
merging for a moment, then isolate,
as they led us to your street, your door,
and up the steps until, inside,
love became articulate: eye, lip, and brow.
When we are shadows watching over shadows,
we will not speak of it but *know*, and turn
again toward each other tenderly,
                    shadow to shadow.

Love's Body

Outside my window a loose branch,
shaped like a shaky *Y*, hangs high
in a tree half-dead, half-alive.
Obedient to form, it mirrors the merely
human: two skeletal legs covered with bark,
with knots at the knees and twigs
forking out where each foot should be;
it has no upper torso.
The seasons come and go, they come and go,
and never is the branch swept down
and carried away by rain or snow,
by the force of wind
mindlessly pounding the window.
Instead, it holds to itself
like the mind in meditation
or, bad days,
sways back and forth, back and forth,
the way one does in love when torn in two,
the hidden heartwood
darkening in a word flood of emotion
that asks *why, why,*
no head, no hands, no mouth
to shape a human answer,
as we come and go, come and go,
on a late cold afternoon in November,
branch to leafless
branch with each other, Nature breaking me
down into something new
I artlessly suffer to tell you.

"Ever-Changing Landscape"

LADEW TOPIARY GARDENS:
MONKTON, MARYLAND

Merciful, yet without mercy,
four hounds pursue a fox,
a horse and rider following
close behind, across a lawn
as broad as it is long.
The fox will never be caught
but never rest, the horse
and rider never quite clear
the fence, no matter
how many days and nights
the chase goes on. Everything
here arrested, out of time,
maintained in trust under
Harvey Ladew's benevolent,
posthumous direction—
a manor house that nobody
lives in, a studio, and high
hedges of yew clipped
into rosettes and curlicues
that form a maze defining
fifteen formal gardens.
From a footbridge, the iris
garden is asymetrical,
"poetic" like a haiku, a junk
with a red sail floating
on a winding man-made stream,
a leafed giraffe nibbling
at a tree—or trying to

since its neck can't reach—
while Buddha contemplates
the scene with serene good humor.

It starts to rain, big drops
spattering the mirror
surface of the Great Bowl,
once Ladew's oval swimming pool.
We hurry through the Garden of Eden,
a leafless canopy of apple
and crab-apple trees leading
to statues of Adam and Eve,
fallen apples at their feet,
to the gun range, a topiary zoo
of swans, unicorns, and lyrebirds,
some of the topiary slightly
in disorder, "in the rough,"
looking as if it hasn't been
clipped for months, perhaps because
it's late in the fall and visitors
are unusual this time of year,
the gardens so impoverished, *bare*,
so few flowers left, the air
so wet. It's raining harder.

We come to the Tivoli,
a little white teahouse
with gingerbread trim where Ladew

entertained his lady friends,
standing like a frail hallucination
at the end of the path.
The door, unlocked, swings in
to an octagonal room
with pink chair, pink loveseat—
overstuffed but threadbare—
a fireplace and two tables.
The room and furniture smell dank,
shut-up, the white paint
on the ceiling and walls
peeling in long flakes, the warped
floorboards covered with mildew.
On one table, a jardiniere
with an effusive personality—
a lady with rouged cheeks
and abundant flowered hat,
lips pursed in a Cupid's bow
like Mary Pickford's. On the table
opposite, old *Saturday Reviews*
from the 1940s with reviews of books
we always meant to read and never
got to. We sit on the loveseat,
glad to be out of the rain,
imagining a real cup of tea,
a fire in the empty fireplace,
noticing the picture window
has a big gold frame around it

and a tiny label underneath:
"Ever-Changing Landscape"
by Harvey Ladew. Another
of his jokes, his clichéd way
of seeing so determinedly
"old hat" it's somehow charming.
The window looks out beyond
the hedgerows of topiary
to a row of hills, mostly brown,
with occasional orange and gold
highlights, muted, subdued
like the day, like the sky,
unchanging to our eye, and yet
if we sat here long enough,
certainly the scene *would* change,
as we would, nature stripping
the hills bare, then coloring them
green again, a cycle to be
depended on like night and day.
The easy certainty of nature
opposed to the artifice of topiary,
the hills' "ever-changing dream"
juxtaposed with swans and unicorns
that have to be constantly
pruned and clipped to keep them
recognizable, unchanging.
Already it's late afternoon,
the view from the window

darkening like an old oil painting,
hills flattening to shadow,
rain taking the edge off
everything. Time *is* fleeting,
a platitude I think Ladew
would agree with. In a minute,
regretfully, we'll leave the Tivoli,
the empty-headed jardiniere,
and the view, all intersecting.
Nature will have its way.
The topiary, left unclipped
all winter, growing into
what it wants to be.